DROGHEDA RHYMES

and other verses

By

Ann Crilly

Composed in Drogheda by a Drogheda resident and many of them are about the town

ISBN: 978-1905451-61-6

A CIP catalogue for this book is available from the National Library.

The author acknowledges with thanks the receipt of an Arts Award from Drogheda Borough Council which has helped in the production of this work.

This book was published in cooperation with
Choice Publishing & Book Services Ltd, Ireland
Tel: 041 9841551 Email: info@choicepublishing.ie
www.choicepublishing.ie

Ann Crilly has been writing verses all her life. These are just a few of her entire product. Many other poems about Drogheda have appeared in her book *'The City of the Churches'*. She has also published a book of humorous verses about her music teaching called *'Interludes'*.

Other books by Ann Crilly have been *'The Paschal Fire'* short stories, *'Words Of The Master'* gospel quotations and songs, *'Witness'* gospel stories from a different angle, and *'Light and Shade'* short stories.

COVER PICTURE
MILLMOUNT

The great mound on which the 19th century Martello Tower now rests is considered to be of prehistoric origin. It is said to be the burial place of Amergin the poet warrior, son of Mileseus, who was killed in battle on the adjacent plain of Magh Breagh in Co. Meath about 1000 B.C.

Index

Nature

General

Prologue

Broadcast on Evan Boland's Poetry Programme, Radio Eireann

An Amateur Writer's Prayer

Lord, make this pen a key to fit my mind.
My long imprisoned thoughts fret in their cage.
I must release them, give them parts to speak,
Costumed in ink upon this paper stage.

Even jails do not have silence bars.
I have such songs to sing, such tales to tell,
Poems to recite that burn my inner soul
And sear my conscience like the flames of hell.

I want to write of love, of hate and fear.
Of literary oaks, I have the seed.
But I must sow: Lord give my pen the power.
Then may I touch the hearts of those who read.

Verses Featuring Drogheda

First published in
The Drogheda Independent

Greenbatter Farm - Ballad

Greenbatter was once an area outside the town (The name taken from the Irish means the sunny road).

The leafy lane that curved outside the town
And brought me to a country paradise,
Has now became a tar and concrete road
Leading to new estates of every size.

Where is the field where Dolly used to graze;
The horse that powered the milkman's daily round?
The long low barn, that housed the dairy herd
In winter months, is nowhere to be found.

For wonder garden, once the farmer's pride,
Haven for singing birds, I search in vain.
There are poor imitations set in rows.
We will never see its like again.

Lovely perfumed creepers trailed its walls.
Roses hung in arches o'er each walk.
There were secret nests in every hedge
And glorious blossoms on each flowering stalk.

In the haggard massive cocks of hay
Were stored against the winter's hungry
cold.
Bringing home the crop on bumpy slides
Was fun for all the children, young and old.

Sitting by the hearth when day was done
We watched the wood smoke rise up to the
stars.
Then folklore and old legends were retold
And there were pictures in the blazing spars.

Alas! The leafy lane is now no more.
What have we got instead of hawthorn
sprays?
Satellite dishes! Burglar alarms!
These make us long for simpler, happy days.

Yes all is changed. The busy farm is gone.
The growing town has wiped it clean away.
But I can close my eyes and see it still
And smell the sweetness of its new-mown
hay.

Drogheda The Tailor

Magdalene tower points towards the sky,
It's broken needle's Gothic eye
Threaded with history.

'Neath Millmount's spool the river weaves,
It's blade through city fabric cleaves
Patterned in mystery.

The town has spread its cloth on land,
Beyond the walls that used to stand
Around it's verge.

The town clock's thimble crowns the street,
Where warf and woof of commerce meet
In merchant serge.

This is the town where Cromwell's fire,
Consumed the refugee thronged spire
On Peter's hill.

A town whose worsted yarn and mine,
On time's immortal loom entwine
And ever will.

**Drogheda And
The Two Olivers**

Two Olivers have left their marks upon
Your ancient stones.
One we recall with terror while we
Laud the other's bones.
The Plunkett family's landed roots
Sprang from a fertile plain.
Cromwell was the rebel son who
Caused his country pain.

One worked to save a 'Kingdom' and
Divisions tried to heal.
The other overthrew a King and ruled
With fists of steel.
He killed for power. But victory just
Lasted for a day.
While the martyr lives forever, teaching us
A better way.

Walking Down The Green Ballad

Not so very long ago, before the 'family car',
When people were contented with not
travelling very far,
On many a sunny evening, not yet captives
of a screen,
The citizens of Drogheda went walking
down the Green.

It was a very pleasant place, to pass some
part of day,
Chatting with the neighbours, whom they
met upon the way.
They watched the lazy river Boyne, flow
stately as a queen,
When the citizens of Drogheda went
walking down the Green.

The fishermens' small rowing boats had
moorings by the wall.
They rocked beside their barrel buoys with
the tidal rise and fall.
And nets were left a-drying, hung on
roadside trees between,
When the citizens of Drogheda went
walking down the Green.

Across the Boyne, at the rowing club the folk
would pause and gaze,
At the Annual Regatta, it with colour was
ablaze.

But on each Summer evening the rowing
was so keen,
When the citizens of Drogheda went
walking down the Green.

They watched the trade and commerce of a
busy thriving port.
As many vessels came and went with flags of
every sort,
Cranes rattled on the dock-side beyond the
Viaduct's screen,
When the citizens of Drogheda went
walking down the Green.

Some came with prams, and children
played so happy on the grass.
And sometimes students brought their
books and watched the steam trains pass.
In dusk, sometimes romance would bloom
as cupid struck unseen,
When the citizens of Drogheda went
walking down the Green.

The Pope's Visit

Pope John Paul came to Drogheda,
Well, he was very near.
He flew right over this old place
To a field at Killineer.

He did not walk along our streets,
Within the boundary's rim.
But that did not really matter,
The town went out to him.

Upon his bended knees he prayed
For calm and lasting peace.
He asked that all conflicts would end,
That hate and fear would cease.

Thank God that now has come about,
When foes at last agreed
That the common good of all is more
Important than their need.

The Pope he came to Drogheda
And looked at us with pity.
The outcome of his visit brought
Some blessings on our city.

The crowd that surged around him
Heard what he had to say,
And knew that they experienced
A very special day.

The Bridge Beside The Ford Ballad

Way back in 1649, there was a day so sad
When Drogheda was invaded and the outcome was so bad.
They still call it Cromwell's Mount, from where his cannon roared,
Before he took the city, the Bridge beside the Ford.

His army charging past the Dales tore the defences down,
And Cromwell's cruel invaders went racing through the town,
They did not temper victory with mercy or kind word,
That day so very long ago, at the Bridge beside the Ford.

Some townsfolk fled for refuge within St. Peter's spire.
So the jubilant attackers came and set the tower on fire.
Trapped up in the belfry as the smoke and blazes soared.
The natives died in agony near the Bridge beside the Ford.

What Cromwell wrote to Dublin, the imagination stretches.
'This was God's righteous judgement upon these barbarous wretches.'

So Drogheda suffered badly at the hands of such a horde,
When the troopers led by Cromwell took the Bridge beside the Ford.

Millmount And Amergin

(Amergin was a warrier poet who is supposed to be buried at Millmount)

You wielded weapons for a frantic cause,
In distant battles waged o'er land or stock.
No one cares now if you lost or won,
Or if you gave your life for beast or rock.

They'd take more notice now of what you
wrote,
Describing how you lived or how you
thought.
The pen can be more powerful than the
sword,
And make more impact than a battle fought.

No matter how you lived or how you died.
Your father held you in such high esteem,
He built this tomb for you beside the Boyne,
Towering up above the gentle stream.

It is a landmark seen from all around,
A tribute to a soldier, poet and prince.
Three thousand years since you've been laid
to rest;
And you have stood on guard there ever
since.

<u>Verses From The Boyne Valley</u>

<u>Solstice At Newgrange</u>

We wonder at the men who built this place,
Experts in the pre-historic age,
We marvel at their accuracy, design,
At the direction of some super sage.

Their task was huge, impressive their
success.
But we must also wonder at the power,
Which even after many thousand years
Delivers sunrise to the very hour.

The Dreamer
John Boyle O' Reilly

First published in
The Drogheda Independent

You dreamt of the peaceful river
In the valley of your youth.
Where you played, an ancient people
Had forever searched for truth.
You dreamt of a peaceful future
When all men would be free.
And you strove by your words
And actions towards this reality.

You never returned to your valley.
That longing was locked in your heart.
The chains that you struggled to loosen,
At least some have fallen apart.
Now men are just grasping the knowledge
That they are all part of a team.
And the future must surely be brighter
Because men like you had a dream.

The Ballad Of The Maiden Tower

(The Maiden tower stands at the mouth of the Boyne)

There stands the tower beside the sea,
Where waves can wash each ancient wall.
An aid to ships in by-gone days,
It beckoned with it's beacon tall.

They lit a bonfire up above,
To blaze a message near and far.
When viewed at dark, with rising tide,
It guided sailors o'er the bar.

The lovers met beneath its shade,
He heading for a distant shore.
On his return they would be wed.
"I will be back" he swore once more.

"There is my flag upon the mast.
Now keep a vigil o'er the brine,
And when my ship comes into view
This flag will show, my heart's still thine".

The maiden watched. The time slipped by.
Lonely, she climbed the stony way.
In rain and wind, in sun and shower,
She scanned the ocean day by day.

Her hopes began to fade away,
As time went by and no return.
Doubts began to cloud her mind,
And for her sweetheart, she did yearn.

Then at last, the day it came.
His ship appeared upon the tide.
She saw it from her vantage point
And hope within her heart revived.

But wait there is no flag on show,
No ensign flying o'er the sail.
Her lover's heart was hers no more.
The maiden gave a fearsome wail.

Straight from the battlements she leapt,
Down to the jagged rocks below.
Her body broken as her heart,
Lay where the Boyne's deep waters flow.

Her lover hearing 'Land ahoy'
Still unaware of cruel fate,
Came up on deck to take the helm.
Ran up the flag; alas too late!

The Blackbird of Slane

To Francis Ledwidge,
Poet of the Boyne Valley

Sweet bird, a jewel in perfect background
set,
Where Patrick lit the paschal fire you flew;
Your bubbling song along the banks of
Boyne,
More beautiful than each exquisite view.

What pity that your season was so short.
You fell in Flanders with war-broken wing,
Pouring your blood upon the alien soil.
Why must a blackbird only sing in Spring?

Francis Ledwidge

On reading his poems.

You dipped your pen into the wide sky
And all its sunset colours glowed in words.
In short sentences you clasped forever
The pastoral beauty of a hill, a field.
Mere pages show your heart's tender
reaction
To gentle birdsong and the beat of wings.
I read these verses and the soft rain
Falls on my face and I can breathe again
Air that is pure yet so intoxicating,
Sweet with the perfume of the wild rose.
The humble flowers of countryside and lane
Are people now, they whisper and they cry.
Through your observant eyes I watch the
stars.
I hear with you the music of the night.
Because you choose to write, I feel your love
For all of God's creation, I share your joy.

Music Verses

Prize Winner in a Drogheda Arts Centre Poetry Competition.

Flead Ceoil

There is the skirl of battle in the pipes,
The wild lament of famine, 'neath the bow.
A nation's pulse throbs in the borhan's skin.
The flute lisps tales of heartbreak long ago.

From harps are plucked the saddest songs of all:
Defeat, destruction from invading hordes.
Personal woes and national despair
Vie for the favours of their troubled cords.

But there is laughter too in jig and reel.
The country folk dance out each tune they call.
And travelling bards sing of impassioned love
In chimney nook and ancient castle hall.

The rustic with the fiddle 'neath his chin,
And airs he learnt at his father's knee
Reaches deep into a people's heart
Draws from the very Spring of history.

Youth Orchestra

You bring the breath of Spring to music's
world,
Clothing its countryside with new life now.
A crochet christening shawl of buds enfolds
Even Beethoven's massive oaken brow.

The bright sunlight of promise permeates,
And wakens hope in every woodland park.
Stirred by this season's fresh simplicity,
Each listening heart becomes a soaring lark.

Concerto

Rich tapestry of sound, alive with light,
Bright flashing brass, more sombre cello
brown,
Pastel shades of woodwind, piccolo green,
Ice-blue notes of oboe pouring down.

Design intricate as a man can make,
The weaving tunes, rich blended chords
display.
A melody parades in every guise
That key and tone and tempo can array.

The whole pulsates and throbs with zestful
life
My heart beats with it, surges on its tide,
Drinks in the alcohol that music brews,
Loses all contact with the world outside.

This has completeness that the soul desires,
Wakens emotions, wooes, suspends, fulfils.
Soothing relief comes at its cadences,
Joyful release as a cadenza trills.

Here is a ticket to the furthest stars
Adventure, thrills upon sonorous seas.
My soul sings out, tuned to eternal song
And finds God's fingers on the ivory keys.

Sea Symphony

The icy fingers of an angry sea
Flash along the keyboard of the shore.
Hear them pound out strange rhythms on
the strand
And rouse to a crescendo the muffled roar,
Of troubled waters rushing all confused.
Where the tall cliffs stand the foam gleams
white.
Echoing the crashing chords of surf
The rocks along the pier stand black as
night.

How different it is when you know how
lovingly
The Summer waves caress the warm brown
sands
When the music of the sea is soft and gentle,
And quiet is the motion of its hands.
Now, the great unseen conductor takes his
stand,
Guides with unknown beat, unknown key.
The voice of every rock and wave and wind
Unite in one great symphony of the sea.

The Composer

Two hundred years ago, by candlelight,
In icy garret quill in hand he wrote.
His world was small. His work was infinite.
He set jewels in position note by note.

He wrote, perhaps, because he had to write.
His lifetime brought no fortune, little fame.
How poor the world would be without him
now,
When millions reverently love his name.

He might have heard his symphony played
once.
Seldom his music soul could breathe fresh
air.
It drew its life from some eternal font,
And even in its triumph fought despair.

We can sit back in comfort, press a switch.
And flood our homes with his great inner
joy.
Even his most anguished cries of pain,
Become a public show, perhaps a toy.

I hear his work in stereophonic sound.
A ninety piece orchestra in my room.
But e'en before it vibrated air,
He heard its secrets in the mind's quiet
womb.

<u>To Music</u>

Music come creeping softly to my ears
Then sweep your great waves o'er my
conscious mind,
That I may sink deep in your swirling
waters,
In their unchartered depths consolance find.

Lost in your aqueous world, harmonious
tides
Immerse my whole being in a vibrant glow.
Where nought else matters but the taste of
sound,
I drift where sweet melodic currents flow.

Hold me within your marine spell entranced
Till I am beached on silence's stark shore,
Tired yet refreshed, but never satisfied,
My hungry ears forever long for more.

Bedtime

I like to lie awake at night
And hear rain fingers strum
With castanets of brittle leaves
Or roof tiles for a drum.

The drain is like a gurgling flute
With liquid notes played low.
Across the television mast
The west wind draws a bow.

I like to lie awake and hear
The elements at play,
The music lifting up my soul
And helping me to pray.

The Street Musician

He fashions strings of jewels and casts them
in the air.
Endows each gem with passion but no one
seems to care.
He weaves designs so intricate yet with a
delicate poise.
Wonderous how they can endure against the
city's noise.

The traffic rumbles by him, a throbbing
noise like pain.
His shafts of sound remind us of sunshine
on ripe grain.
The dreadful drills of road works play havoc
with his art,
Though there are few who listen, he reaches
every heart.

He draws deep breath and pours more notes
out of his soul and flute.
They hang, just music bubbles, above the
busy route.
His cap upon the pavement has gathered
little pay,
But he has brought some happiness to many
souls today.

Space Songs

Moonshot

First published in The Sunday Independent

(An astronaut speaks)

Look at the moon! I was there!
Coasting through space, it was always day.
I watched the crescent earth decline,
Shrinking, falling, far away.

Intricate scientific skill
Shot me higher than any man,
Design, precision, but surpassed
By the universal plan.

I reached man's stepping-stone to stars.
Swiftly I scanned its arid girth,
Stared at infinity and thought
How insignificant is Earth.

Moon Exploration

Written before the Moon Landings

Man wooes this virgin of the skies.
First serenades her from afar,
Then tentatively takes her hand
Compares her glories to a star.

Will she rebuke him? None can say.
Or clasp him in a warm embrace.
Will she disdain to hear his suit
And send him earthward in disgrace?

Like any lover, man may pine.
Will his desire be ever sated?
Only through time, research and skill
Can nuptial strange be consummated.

Apollo 13

An odyssey astray, man reaches far.
A globe slips from his tentative embrace.
Now all his hopes and fears are clasped
within
A tiny speck in space.

May it not a satellite tomb become,
Or human meteorite in flaming kill.
Three hearts still beat in cursed translunar
flight
And the world's heart stands still.

The New World. Moon Walk

No gentle foliage shades the sun.
Roses or orchids there are none.
No butterfly makes fickle fun
On painted wing;
No tide flows there. The seas are dry.
A blue orb hangs in darkened sky.
No streams or lakes or springs are nigh,
And no birds sing.

Is this a Sodom or Gomorrah
Suspended high, a spacious horror,
In all its grim unshriven squalor,
On Satan's wing?
Punished for prehistoric sin,
Cut far away from earthly kin,
Forever doomed to silent spin
Where no birds sing.

Perhaps man dreams that he can mine.
Somewhere illusive metals shine,
Moongold and lunar diamonds fine,
For earthly ring.
A thousand dead volcanoes pout
On a sphere destroyed by drought.
What can man find? There is no doubt,
That no birds sing.

Maybe gems unheard-of, new,
Mineral wealth to grace a few,
Can magnetise each daring crew
Orbiting.
What use? what cost? an epic flight
To reach this citadel of night,
To find a world in such a plight
That no birds sing.

Aliens

Are there folk out there in stellar orbit,
Who trace our solar system in their sky?
Are they land-locked on their distant
planets,
Or have they got ability to fly?

Are they cavemen worshipping strange
spirits,
Or super scientists with extra skill?
Can they bridge the vast expanse between
us?
Have they the technology or will?

Maybe they've already made their visits,
And looked upon our troubles with dismay.
Maybe they've decided in their wisdom,
It's better that they keep us far away.

Sea Songs

A Song Of The Sea

Away! Away! on the surging sea
Where the sea birds call, where the winds
blow free
Away! Away on the rolling wave
Who speaks of death or the sailor's grave?

There's a salty breeze to fill the sail
Who fears the storm or the threatening
gale?
The ship's alive in the grip of the tide.
She leaps the billows and waves that ride
Along the deep. She spurns the spray.
And drenched with foam she wins the day.
With the sea before and the wind behind
There's a spirit here that you'll never find,
A spirit of freedom, you'll never rein
On the rooted hills. A wilder vein
Than that which throbs on a country lea.
So Away! Away! on the surging sea.

The Old Woman By The Sea

I hear the mass bell ringing. Its sound
comes o'er the bay,
I hear the people passing but here alas, I
stay.

My home's become a prison. My bones are
just a cage,
Barred in with aching muscles and chained
with twisted age.

The road from my small cottage winds
round beside the sea.
Oh many times I've walked it when the mass
bell called to me.

I remember as a youngster, when I played
along the shore,
The warnings, not to bring the sand onto the
chapel floor.

I remember as a colleen I met him on the
way
Arm in arm we'd wander on the road to
pray.

I remember as a mother, keeping a wary eye
On the laughing children when the tide was
high.

Years are quick in passing. The road itself
grew long.
The hill up to the chapel is cambered for the
strong.

I hear the mass bell ringing. It's sound
comes o'er the strand
Soon I will leave my prison, go to a better
land.

I'll pass the bridge at Seafield, the rocks at
Carrickree,
And in my final journey the bell will toll for
me.

Titanic Contrasts

The fastest? Yet so slow it ne'er reached
port.
The marvellous launching then the dismal
hurt.
The largest? Yet so small naught could they
find,
But only tiny lifeboats left behind.
These did not match the many nor the few,
The lost, the found, the passengers, the
crew.
The safest? Yet so dangerous to all.
So few could answer its last Mayday call.
The richest? Yet so poor – to save, unable.
Now steerage tickets sit at captain's table.
A rendezvous with ice melts down all class.
They all become as one in ocean's mass.
First voyage, also last – so short, yet long.
The world cannot forget how weak the
strong.

To The Sea

Some lines written on the beach.

I come like an ancient pilgrim to your
shrine,
Reverently worshipping.
Standing in awe before your vast power,
With humble admiration.
I know you do not listen to my prayers
Though I bond with your spirit.
In your calm I feel such restfulness,
Peace and sweet tranquillity,
In your passion such exhilaration,
Responding to your surging strength.
Your role as idol means you can demand
Great sacrifices – offerings.
Those who challenge you always depend
Upon your moods and meagre mercy.
I keep my distance, like the publican,
Burning a candle in my heart.
But I know that even you have a greater
master
Who walked upon your Galilean waves
And even in the raging tempest spoke
Commanding you to instant quiet.

The Seashell

Tiny gem from ocean's crown
With delicately spiralled whorl,
Discarded on a lonely strand,
Lined with lustrous shades of pearl.

A masterpiece in miniature
Perfection scaled to fine degree;
When you hid beneath the waves
What eye appraised your symmetry?

The hand that wrought your lovely shape
And picked your tints from rainbow hue,
Can fashion spiritual jewels
Within each mind admiring you.

You had your use to hold a life
Concealed in crustacean array;
Poor shapeless body now dissolved
In briny liquid washed away.

When this dull tissue too is gone,
May I bequeath a written shell –
Thoughts calcified in beauteous folds
As yours, to hold hearts in a spell.

Pot - Shot

The gull, a ballerina poised
In mid pas seul on aeolian board,
Then effortlessly glides upstage;
A terpsichorean feat encored.

Backcloth of coastal mountain scene
Dims behind its beauteous motion.
A fairy shape with ease performs
A choreography of ocean.

A shot rings out. The music stops.
The dancer plummets like a stone
Sprawled on the pier, its minute brain
Seeps through its shattered case of bone.

The marksman slings his rifle back,
And turns away. He feels no shame.
He'd shot a gull, at ninety yards.
A great day's sport! Fantastic aim!

Religious Rhymes

Christmas Light

It flickers on wax tapers in the churches,
In welcoming windows on the festive eve.
Glows in the faces of the little children,
In eyes of those who give and who receive.

It warms the hearts of many, sad and lonely,
Even through wars and trials it shines afar.
How does it light so constantly undimming?
Because God gave it radiance from the star.

The Carpenter Of Nazareth

The Carpenter was busy at his bench,
With steady hands he plied his chosen
trade.
As shavings fell around his sandalled feet,
Did he think back on other things He made?

As He prepared the lintel of a door,
Did He remember then the start of time,
How He built the hills and split the seas
And raised all life from prehistoric slime?

As He picked the timbers for each task,
And matched their grain with ever loving
care,
Did He recall how he designed the stars,
Laid out their paths and set the suns aglare?

He who made the lily and the rose
Stopped to make the humble bench and
stool.
He who mapped the vast extremes of space
Laboured with common axe and sliding
rule.

When He crossed the heavy planks of wood,
And drove the big nails home with master's
skill.
Did he think then of business yet to do,
Gethsemane and then to Calvary Hill?

Christmas Eve

Let us bring gifts to Bethlehem tonight,
O'er land and sea our humble presents bear;
In the crib behind the crowded inn
We will leave them for the infant sleeping
there.

A gift of gold; A tribute to a king!
Bring all our earthly treasures great and
small.
We will offer them to this mostly gentle
child,
A prince of heaven, monarch over all.

A gift of frankincense; His priestly right !
Let our prayers rise as incense to His throne
Making a thurible of every heart,
Burning with love within for Him alone.

A gift of myrrh; A bitter scented spice!
We bring it too, our sufferings and pain.
Joined with His cross, His noble sacrifice,
Our tears and sorrows cannot be in vain.

Let us bring gifts to Bethlehem tonight,
Magi and shepherds join in pilgrim ride.
Like them we come, the newborn to adore,
With gifts for Him this holy Christmas-tide.

Christmas Communion

The choir had sung the Christmas hymn of
peace,
As I went to the table of the Lord,
My heart and mind troubled by many
things,
"Master! I am not worthy. Say the word".

I thought about the crib at Bethlehem.
The priest raised up the host before my face.
I took the tiny Infant in my arms
And went back, oh so gently, to my place.

War And Peace

Peace 1998
(In Relation to the North)

Peace hovers now on delicate wings,
Beating the air, silently, softly.
It comes like the ceasing of violet pain;
In numbing shock, in frozen feeling.
Its sedative charm thinly masks
The primitive terrors, the stark recall;
The losses, the gains; the balancing powers
That drive yet brake, unite yet sunder.
It comes we pray, in hope, to stay.
Can we dare hold its fragile fabric,
Measure its worth within our hearts
And, forgiving, cling to it forever.

Exorcist

First published in The Sunday Independent

Forthwith, we command, go evil spirit go!
From this unfortunate prey, you have
dragged so low
We have seen the signs of your satanic
being,
The convulsive bomb outrage, the
intimidator's spleen.

Help us, our shepherd slave, saint of
Slemish and Slane
Add your strong voice to ours, banish the
snakes again.
Depart, vile demon force, from this our
shattered land
Go evil spirit, go! In Christ's name we
command.

10th April Good Friday 1998

Who fears to speak – a battle cry
 of old
Becomes a legend when the tale
is told.
The full moon raises tides of hope
and fear.
Men cling to fragments that they
hold so dear.
The pike is missing now and in
its place
The powerful pen unites a
stubborn race.
At Easter-tide when life is all
renewed,
We overcome each deathly hate
and feud.
Who fears to speak as ancient
troubles cease.
Who fears to speak, to shout, to cry
for peace?

Dial N.Y 9.11.01

(After the Twin Towers bombing, the victims' mobile phones were heard ringing for some time by the recuers)

"Dad! When are you coming home?
Buster's waiting at the door".
Another message not received,
For dad's not coming any more.

"Darling, tell me you're all right.
We saw the horror on T.V.
Hope that you have gotten out.
Love you Darling. Please ring me".

"Buddy tell us what's gone wrong.
Heard a newsflash! Can't be real!
We've lost contact with your line,
And we need to close the Boston deal".

"Paddy, we've just got your call.
Fire fighting crews are on their way.
You're on the 92nd floor!
Gee! Get out fast now. Don't delay".

"I've been ringing you all day.
I feel you simply must survive.
But I'm getting no reply.
Answer please. Show you're alive".

Omagh

Over the very brink,
No lower can they sink,
Who engineered this deed.

The ultimate in pain!
It cannot come again;
No right ! No cause! No need!

The devil's had his day.
The guiltless victims pay
As do their stricken kin.

What can they ever do,
Who planned! who caused! who knew!
To purge this grievous sin?

Peace Talks

Conferences and meetings stagger on.
Heads of state haggle, weeks slip by.
The fire of hunger smoulders through the
land
And people die.

Disputes about priorities, agendas,
Bring deadlock to the tables of the high.
As they argue, the guns keep spitting
murder,
More people die.

Walkout and breakdowns come in quick
succession
Generals gamble and some statesmen lie.
Children and women weep as food grows
shorter.
More people die.

Delegations fail to find agreement,
As they deliberate the warplanes fly.
Bombs burst and scatter poverty's
possessions
More people die.

Rulers fear a loss of face or fortune,
Yield not an inch and give no reason why.
While knives are cutting deep in human
tissue,
More people die.

Some men believe they talk to save a nation.
Lands without folk their eloquence deny.
Pain and famine sit at many tables.
More people die.

Oh Lord give hearts to men who trust in
battles
So deaf they cannot hear the suffering cry.
What's to be written in the book of
judgement.
When statesmen die?

The Wolves Of War

The wolves of war are howling in the hills
Blood runs ice cold as each cry strikes the
ear.
Like angry seas around an isle they crowd
Sometimes they sound afar and then quite
near.

The wolves of war are running through the
streets,
Growling and snarling, hungry mouths
agape.
Snapping, biting, seeking to destroy.
Satan concealed in every ugly shape.

The wolves of war are whimpering round
the walls,
Sniffing at thresholds. Paws at windows
tear.
Their eyes are burning coals. Their
streaming fangs
Send clouds of steam into the frigid air.

The wolves of war are scraping at the doors
Hurtling their bodies at each shaking frame.
They would devour our children and our
stock.
These raging beasts can never be made
tame.

We cannot hide, we cannot get away
Pack after pack howl out the hideous knell
Oh God ! Bring Spring of peace to the
besieged
And chain these wolves of war deep down in
Hell.

On Writing

Word Mason

I work with words, hewn out of books and
tongues.
I lay them carefully and match their size,
Using the very mortar of my soul
To bind each course and make the structure
rise.

I pick these stones to suit the task on hand.
Some words are polished smooth by use and
time.
Some have the jagged edge of virgin rock,
And others have peculiar shape and rhyme.

I must carry hod and work with trowel,
And mix the concrete too with patient
spade.
There is no journeyman to help my task
For building words is such a lonely trade.

Some day I will build castles, mansions,
towers,
Raise walls and battlements and turrets
grand.
Then hope that folk will see the tradesman's
skill
And that my work the test of time will stand.

But now at some small monuments I strive
To learn my trade, and show how grace of stone
Lies in the strength and beauty of mere words.
I pick each rock and build each poem alone.

<u>Envy</u>

I know that I've written a novel, though it
did not go very far.
Perhaps with the proper production it might
have become quite a star.
I know that I simply love writing and my
hopes in that way are so wild.
I long to become a best seller, but you've
given birth to a child.

I know that I've written some verses and in
them I've laid out my soul.
It gives me some small satisfaction to read
them back partly or whole.
In them I've given expression to when I was
happy or riled.
But think of the wonderous achievement
that you've given birth to a child.

I know that at plays I've endeavoured to
bring my poor thoughts to the stage.
But words cannot make a life longer nor
hand on some genes to new age.
Mere sentences cannot endeavour to pass
on a line undefiled.
While you have secured a succession, for
you've given birth to a child.

Recipe For A Poem

Gather the grain
In the abundant sheaves of youthfulness
Or glean the ears
Germ ideas in the raw stubble age.
Ferment with thought.
Yeast-like deep contemplation rises,
Malts in the mind.
Distil with the cool worm of philosophy.
Then tightly cask
In cellars of emotional experience.
Finally matured
The potent liquid sparkles in language glass,
Bottled in books.
Now all can share the poet's intoxication
Uncork and drink.

Nature

A Sheltered Snowdrop

I saw the monstrous giants of oak and elm,
With twisted fingers clutching at the sky.
Their naked limbs distorted and entwined
Beat at the air. I heard them moan and
sigh.

I saw the tiny elf of leaf and stem,
So calm and silent, dignified yet frail.
Its tiny waxen chalice purely wrought,
A-nodding quietly to the soaring gale.

The Witching Moon

Darkness has drawn her veils and all is
silent,
When the witching moon climbs the clear
Eastern sky,
Trailing her simmering skirts on the silver
waters
And on the sleeping hills that southward lie.

Higher she climbs and her long flowing
robes
Damp from the glistening waters sweep the
land.
Here with their frills of mist brush past the
trees
And gleam on boughs half-stripped by
Autumn's hand.

They stir while passing the brown crumpled
leaves,
That lie in patterned pools on road and
street.
Quietly she moves on her bewitching way
On silent wings or even noiseless feet.

She casts a silver spell on roof and field,
And on the stars that join her in her ride,
Pausing a while along the river's bank
To cast a sparkling net into its tide.

Softly she treads on her pathway through
the heavens
Until she descends her staircase of the West.
Why does she haunt this land of peace and
darkness,
Transforming night? What is her lonely
quest?

The Kitten

Little cat with purr bewitching,
Roguish eyes that gleam with fun.
Ears and tail forever twitching,
Playful paws that leap and run.

Piece of string! a tempting quarry!
Crazy game with rubber ball.
Now and then a feline flurry,
Down the stairs and through the hall.

Wound-up spring of kitten madness,
Loosed in many spurts of glee.
Show me how, mischievous gladness,
To be young again and free.

The Fledgeling

You stagger on the roadway
Like a drunk crossing the street,
Awkward, bewildered, lost,
Unsure of your truant feet.

Still with your head held high
You listen and make a call.
Help used to come much quicker
Before you had that fall.

Your body's perfect frame
Is streamlined for the skies.
Though there are tufts of fluff
On your head above your eyes.

You may be lost right now,
Or the runway is not clear.
But when the take-off comes,
You'll make it without fear.

You, who stumble now,
Will soon control your fright,
And challenge all the winds
With your great gift of flight.

After A Wild Night

The wind is saddled now.
All night long with hooves a-wing,
It thundered over everything,
And made a fearful row.

It galloped in the sky,
Tossing its mane against the moon,
Trampling the tattered clouds to ruin,
Making the star sparks fly.

It raced o'er every field.
Crushing the grasses to the ground,
Filling the dark with monstrous sound,
Bending all that would yield.

It clattered through the town.
Every door it kicked and pushed,
O'er every roof and yard it rushed,
Nothing could tie it down.

We heard its awful neigh
Echoing in the twisting trees,
Making our chimneys gasp and wheeze.
What did it try to say?

Its bid for freedom past,
Now it trots on gentle rein;
No longer snorting wild with strain.
The wind is saddled at last.

A Glorious Summer's Day

A gypsy bronzed, attired in colours gay
Comes to our door, with spangles in her
hair.
She bears the wisdom of her nomad race
And from a basket vends her trinket ware.

Her shawl of mottled fields is worn with
grace.
There are jewels at her ears and hands.
Her voice and manner tell of warmer climes
For this true Romany comes from distant
lands

We cross her palm with silver, she foretells
A harvest bountiful, a winter grey.
We look around – distraction's brief respite
When we look back, the gypsy's gone away.

Nightmare/Pollution

I dreamt; - strange flowers burst into bloom
And spread their petals far and wide,
Orange, red and mushroom grey.
All living things that touched them died.

I felt the air grow dense and dark.
All the sky was cloud and smoke.
With every breath I inhaled fire
That scorched my lungs and made me
choke.

The waters changed their substance, hue,
In lake and stream and tidal bay.
Then the currents ceased to flow
And stagnant stank of sour decay.

No wind or rain could cleanse the earth
Nature could not restore or heal.
I tried to rouse my drowsy brain
And found I slept not. This was real!

General

Autumn Love

There is a springtime in our lives
When young love buds in every heart,
And blossoms with the riotous flowers
In sunshine when the swallows dart.

The summer deepens and matures
Grows mellow as time melts away.
They say one never can recall
The sparkling passion felt in May.

But if love comes mid golden leaves,
Those feeling the exquisite pain
Can see the dancing daffodils
And hear the blackbird sing again.

Alcock And Brown

(First Men to Fly Across the Atlantic)

Fledgling man, in fragile frigate
Challenged, like migrating swallow,
Perilous winds and cumulus:

In undreamt-of span of flight
Retraced above with stammering pistons
The slower pulse of Brendan's oars.

With frail frame tempted the very airs
That teased Columbus's tacking jib;
Landfall on peat – an ocean bridged.

Adventurous man now, with pinions
Feathered by rocket motors, casts
A cold eye at unblinking stars.

A Life Of Seasons

Spring is the time for sowing,
The time for learning, growing,
The time for dreams and hope for what's to
be.

The Summer re-enforces,
May lead through many courses.
Develops, seals, matures, and sets us free.

The Autumn's time for reaping,
Rejoicing, sometimes weeping,
When we assess what did life really bring.

The Winter's bleak and colder,
We know we've grown older,
Yet wish that we could see another Spring.

My Toys

When I was young, I played with simple toys.
Bright buttons laid in rows became for me
Delph on my dresser, goods within my shop
Or anything else I wanted them to be.

My mother sang each day she combed my hair.
And told me stories 'once upon a time'.
I had a skipping rope, a rubber ball,
A wooden horse pulled by a piece of twine.

The children now have space suits and TV,
Expensive guns and cars and dolls that walk.
They even bring their mobile phones to school
Collect pop records, soon as they can talk.

Their childhood is so short and mine was long.
I can look back on its expanse and dream
That I am young again and make believe
Things are as I want, not as they seem.

Abortion

Baby in a bucket, naked, red,
Victim of a traitorous surgeon's tool.
Destined along with gangrenous guts and
tumours
To become the clinic's incinerator fuel.

Poor shivering sliver of humanity;
No cooing words for you, no favourite toy;
The offal of reneged creation gets
No petticoats or bib, blue for a boy.

Will you haunt the dreams of your
destroyers
Calling 'Ma Ma' in the dreaded night?
You might have been a statesman, priest or
scholar
But a human foetus has no human right.

Birth is the great beginning for us all.
For you, so tiny mite, death came before.
This price you paid for mother's 'right to
choose'!
But I fear that she herself may yet pay more.

Consolation

Ode to a dear departed one.

The blow was sudden, cruel, the pain
transfixed.
Then utter desolation made its claim.
Groping for sanity, I realised
That everything though changed was still
the same.

You and the warm sunlight now are one.
You are the surge of wavelets on a beach,
The sparkling dew drops on the fragile rose
Not distant or remote, not out of reach.

You are the velvet touch of favourite airs,
Laughter of happy children at their play.
You have become part of the lark's song.
Above the heather on an April day.

Even more so you are now within
The very essences of love and truth.
You have forever joined eternal power
Sustaining good, restoring robust youth.

In going, you have stayed, A tragic loss
Became a massive gain to conquer fear.
I know, because in parting we have met
And in a thousand ways you're always here.

Death, The Highwayman

He lurks around wherever traffic moves.
He lies in wait at every hidden bend,
And even on the 'straight' where his friend 'Speed'
Goads on his victims to a sudden end.

He hangs about the roadside taverns
Tilting the drinkers' arms with devilish glee.
"Fill up the glasses" "Here's one for the road"
Then hands the driver the ignition key.

Frost is a member of his robber gang,
Making a ski-run out of every hill
And skating rink of every level stretch.
Fog is often used to shroud a kill.

Beware of heavy foot and shaking hand.
Beware of blinding lights, impatience rife.
This bandit's everywhere, the ambush laid.
He does not want your money but your life.

He does not rest, for any hour can hear
The sickening sound of smashing glass and steel
One careless moment and the price is paid.
Skid marks! and blood on every startled wheel.

A Day

A day is a wakening, a brightening, a
dawning.
A day is a struggle, a conflict, a yawning.
A day is a time for a laugh or a cry,
A day is a time to be born or to die.
A day is for giving and taking and sharing.
A day is for working, and feeding and
wearing.
A day is for making and mending – a chore.
A day is for striving and gaining for more.
A day is a straightening, a twisting, a
bending.
A day is a trading, a borrowing, a lending.
A day is a growing, maturing, an ageing.
A day is for waiting and watching and
waging.
A day is a sunrise, high noon and sundown.
A childhood, a prime time a golden year's
crown.

A day is for loving for bonding and caring.
A day is for hating and fighting and daring.
A day is for learning, for peace or for strife
A day is all powerful.   A day is a life.

Teacher – Dealer In Knowledge

I glean the gold of learning
Jingle each precious coin in pocket brain.
Gloat o'er my riches
Poor though they are to what some others
gain.

This is my treasure trove,
The currency of thought, the stamp of sages.
The stirling quality
Of noble deeds, emotions through the ages.

I do not hoard my wealth,
Such as it is, but give to all who ask
Scatter my alms abroad
Oft by exchange make profit from the task.

So I become more rich
Than millionaires of metal, land or trade.
Their money dwindles fast.
My bullion's worth or value does not fade.

Even what I give, I hold.
It does not lessen. Studies passed along,
Do not change ownership
But to both parties equally belong.

I trade in lines of knowledge
To students I donate with all my heart
I give not just this gold
With every ounce, I give, of self, a part.

<u>Reflection</u>

Today I saw my Mother, though it's been
forty years.
Since they closed her coffin while we
watched in tears.
I saw her coming towards me as I crossed
the street.
She looked so shocked, bewildered as we
moved to meet.

She was a slender woman with hair
becoming grey.
I was surprised that she was dressed in
clothes we wear today.
I stood and stared, astonished. She also
stopped. Alas!
I faced a showroom window with my image
in the glass.

Insomnia

I fish for salmon sleep in pool of night,
Casting my troubled line to seek that prize.
I wait and watch, hoping that from the deep
Somehow, sometime soon my 'catch' will
rise.

My thoughts like children run along the
bank,
Throwing in pebbles that affect my mind.
Ripples of worries chase my prey away,
Dredging up concerns of every kind.

A small boat comes upstream. A novice
rows,
With many splashing efforts to progress.
Thus my future plans disturb the peace
And cause me much anxiety and stress.

A walker going by with dog on lead
Frees the animal to have a swim.
My memory keeps fetching items back,
Just as his pet retrieves the stick for him.

I reel my efforts in. I change the bait.
And pray that all distractions go away,
While the slippery salmon stays within his
stream,
And leaves me anxiously awaiting day.

Dialogue;
The Law And The Itinerant

First published in The Sunday Independent
(Written before the Itinerant Housing Schemes)

"**B**e on your way!"
"The unwelcome voice is the same in
country and town."
"You cannot stay!"
"Though our wee babe is young and the rain
beats down."
"Pack up your tent!"
"Even the rags and sticks make a heavy
load."
"Go! When you're sent!"
"Huddled in donkey's cart on the open
road!"
"Get a move on!"
"Oh for a permanent roof and hearth
aglow."
"You must be gone!"
"Away from the only shelter that we know?"
"Go! Hurry up!"
"A piece of a sack in a gale is not much help"
"You've stayed long enough!"
"Tramping all day, we've not what would
nourish a whelp."
"What's the delay?"
"Our weary bones are aching from cold and
damp."
"Go! When we say!"
"Ah, people in houses are hard on those in a
camp."

Jailbird

On the discovery of a budgie in a prison.

Did you not sing behind the prison bars,
For a bird within a cage is nothing new?
But this is a place of punishment for men,
Not for redundant wings that never flew.

Confined within your cell you knew naught
else,
A prisoner of a prisoner, how absurd.
Stranger still that monstrous hearts of hate
Could feel affection for a tiny bird.

Pope John Paul II

Young people of Ireland, I love you.
You are close to my heart.
You gave me a Cead Mile Failte.
I know we will not drift apart.

Remember me, as you grow older,
As youth changes into old age.
Remember me in all your actions
When I'm gone from this earthly stage.

I had hoped to revisit in Autumn
An Island so fresh and so green,
To pray with you for peace among you.
Regret not, what just might have been.

Young people of Ireland, I love you.
Keep faith, and for all sins atone.
Recall our so wonderful meeting
And that I did not travel alone.

Flick Knives

Drumbeat and torrid night
Youth on the prowl;
Headlamps and neon light
Etch street scene;
Liquid fire burns
In impatient vein;
Vendetta tiger lurks
In jungle brain;
Suddenly springs forth!
Fangs flash bright!
Warm blood flows
Down city drain.

Today

Each day is a gift that we are free to spend.
It comes with dawn and stays to evening's
end
It brings it's joys and laughter, tears and
pain
But we will never have this day again.

So let us live this day with all our heart.
We may be with our loved ones or apart.
We can't waste time on worries or on strife.
The present time is real. This day is life.

The past is gone away. Its course is run
We cannot change it. What is done is done.
The future may hold promises or fear
But it may never come. Today is here.

For some today is an important date.
A landmark in their lives deciding fate.
Others may not note it any way,
But for us all this is a special day.

<u>Learning And Growing</u>

With every bit you learn you grow a little.
Tender shoots appear within your brain.
All types of knowledge help you to expand,
And general information makes a gain.

Fed by curiosity alone
Your stature has increased in every way.
And thus your study of so many things
Will help your mind to flourish day by day.

So eagerly stretch out for further skills.
For all the 'Whys and Wherefores' there is
room,
And hope that some day as you learn and
grow,
The plants within your mind will start to
bloom.

Our Home

This is our home made of much more than
stone
Our own retreat, where we can always hide.
This is our very special place on earth
And if we wish we keep the world outside.

When we're at work or on the busy street
We dream of coming home to peace and
rest.
If we are far away on other shores
It is the place we think about as best.

This is the house for family and friends
We have put everything together here,
Filled all its rooms with memories and love
Built with our lives its very atmosphere.

Pop Idol

The figure glowed with beauty
The people came to stare.
To imitate religiously
The style of dress and hair.

It stood too high to reach
Almost too far to see.
Millions swirled around its base
Intrigued by mystery.

The common hordes paid tribute
Gave homage night and day.
The idol, toppled off its perch
Shattered! 'Twas made of clay.

The Bethlehem Inn-Keeper And Us

"**I** tell you Sir, there's no room at the inn.
My patrons have come from near and far.
I've never been so rushed in all my life.
I'm torn between the dining room and bar.

I'm sorry Sir, I cannot give you room.
Can't you see I'm busy as a bee.
I must attend to all my business chores
And entertain my guests as well, you see.

I tell you Sir, there's no room at the inn.
Emergency or not, I can't give aid.
Try the stable for at least a roof.
Then you're on your own, I am afraid.

I have to see to linen, drinks and food,
And check that staff perform their duties well.
I have a reputation to uphold.
My standards are quite high as all can tell.

I'm sorry Sir, there is no room for you.
I cannot give you any place to stay."

I know that story's really very old,
But it is still appropriate today.

Final Curtain

(Written at the demolition of the local Parish Centre Theatre)

Noises off in the wings, echoes of the past.
Tumbling masonry shows that nothing's
made to last.
Still the memories remain. History takes a
bow,
When the footlights finally fade, there are
no encores now.

On this stage no more will star the famous
or unknown.
All the exits have been made, the farewell
trumpets blown.
As the final curtain falls the drills and
diggers pause,
And we still hear within our minds the well
deserved applause.